"The days are long,
but the years go by so fast..."

This journal...

is a gift to me
and my future generations.

documents the beautiful milestones
in my child's life.

is a reminder: even on the hardest
of days I can find good.

shows me how far I've come
on my parenting journey.

reminds me of my strength
and bravery through hard times.

is proof I am exactly the parent
my child needs.

is encouragement for me on the days
when I feel like nothing is going right.

is for the moments
I always want to remember.

Date: _______________________

Today I want to remember...

____

____

____

____

Date: _______________________

Today I want to remember...

____

____

____

____

Date: _______________________

Today I want to remember...

____

____

____

____

Date: _______________________

Today I want to remember...

____

____

____

____

____

Date: _______________________

Today I want to remember...

____

____

____

____

____

Date: _______________________

Today I want to remember...

____

____

____

____

____

Date: _______________________

Today I want to remember...

____

____

____

____

Date: _______________________

Today I want to remember...

____

____

____

____

Date: _______________________

Today I want to remember...

____

____

____

____

Date: _______________________________

Today I want to remember...

____

____

____

____

Date: _______________________________

Today I want to remember...

____

____

____

____

____

Date: _______________________________

Today I want to remember...

____

____

____

____

Date: _______________________

Today I want to remember...

____

____

____

____

Date: _______________________

Today I want to remember...

____

____

____

____

Date: _______________________

Today I want to remember...

____

____

____

Date: _______________________________

Today I want to remember...

____

____

____

____

Date: _______________________________

Today I want to remember...

____

____

____

____

Date: _______________________________

Today I want to remember...

____

____

____

____

Date: _______________________________

Today I want to remember...

____

____

____

____

____

Date: _______________________________

Today I want to remember...

____

____

____

____

____

Date: _______________________________

Today I want to remember...

____

____

____

____

Date: _______________________

Today I want to remember...

____

____

____

____

Date: _______________________

Today I want to remember...

____

____

____

____

Date: _______________________

Today I want to remember...

____

____

____

____

Date: ___________________________

Today I want to remember...

____

____

____

____

Date: ___________________________

Today I want to remember...

____

____

____

____

____

Date: ___________________________

Today I want to remember...

____

____

____

____

Date: _______________________

Today I want to remember...

____

____

____

____

____

Date: _______________________

Today I want to remember...

____

____

____

____

____

Date: _______________________

Today I want to remember...

____

____

____

____

Date: _______________________________

Today I want to remember...

____

____

____

____

____

Date: _______________________________

Today I want to remember...

____

____

____

____

____

Date: _______________________________

Today I want to remember...

____

____

____

____

Date: _______________________________

Today I want to remember...

____

____

____

____

Date: _______________________________

Today I want to remember...

____

____

____

____

Date: _______________________________

Today I want to remember...

____

____

____

____

Date: _______________________

Today I want to remember...

____

____

____

____

Date: _______________________

Today I want to remember...

____

____

____

____

Date: _______________________

Today I want to remember...

____

____

____

____

Date: ________________________

Today I want to remember...

____

____

____

____

Date: ________________________

Today I want to remember...

____

____

____

____

Date: ________________________

Today I want to remember...

____

____

____

Date: _______________________________

Today I want to remember...

____

____

____

____

____

Date: _______________________________

Today I want to remember...

____

____

____

____

____

Date: _______________________________

Today I want to remember...

____

____

____

____

Date: _______________________

Today I want to remember...

____

____

____

____

Date: _______________________

Today I want to remember...

____

____

____

____

____

Date: _______________________

Today I want to remember...

____

____

____

____

Date: _______________________________

Today I want to remember...

____

____

____

____

Date: _______________________________

Today I want to remember...

____

____

____

____

Date: _______________________________

Today I want to remember...

____

____

____

____

Date: _______________________

Today I want to remember...

____

____

____

____

____

Date: _______________________

Today I want to remember...

____

____

____

____

____

Date: _______________________

Today I want to remember...

____

____

____

____

Date: ___________________________

Today I want to remember...

____

____

____

____

____

Date: ___________________________

Today I want to remember...

____

____

____

____

____

Date: ___________________________

Today I want to remember...

____

____

____

____

Date: _______________________________

Today I want to remember...

____

____

____

____

Date: _______________________________

Today I want to remember...

____

____

____

____

Date: _______________________________

Today I want to remember...

____

____

____

Date: _______________________

Today I want to remember...

____

____

____

____

Date: _______________________

Today I want to remember...

____

____

____

____

Date: _______________________

Today I want to remember...

____

____

____

Date: _______________________________

Today I want to remember...

____
____
____
____

Date: _______________________________

Today I want to remember...

____
____
____
____

Date: _______________________________

Today I want to remember...

____
____
____
____

Date: _______________________

Today I want to remember...

____

____

____

____

Date: _______________________

Today I want to remember...

____

____

____

____

Date: _______________________

Today I want to remember...

____

____

____

____

Date: ___________________________

Today I want to remember...

____

____

____

____

Date: ___________________________

Today I want to remember...

____

____

____

____

Date: ___________________________

Today I want to remember...

____

____

____

____

Date: _______________________

Today I want to remember...

____

____

____

____

____

Date: _______________________

Today I want to remember...

____

____

____

____

Date: _______________________

Today I want to remember...

____

____

____

____

Date: _______________________________

Today I want to remember...

____

____

____

____

Date: _______________________________

Today I want to remember...

____

____

____

____

____

Date: _______________________________

Today I want to remember...

____

____

____

____

Date: _______________________

Today I want to remember...

____

____

____

____

Date: _______________________

Today I want to remember...

____

____

____

____

Date: _______________________

Today I want to remember...

____

____

____

Date: _______________________

Today I want to remember...

____

____

____

____

Date: _______________________

Today I want to remember...

____

____

____

____

Date: _______________________

Today I want to remember...

____

____

____

____

Date: _______________________

Today I want to remember...

____

____

____

____

____

Date: _______________________

Today I want to remember...

____

____

____

____

____

Date: _______________________

Today I want to remember...

____

____

____

____

Date: _______________________

Today I want to remember...

____

____

____

____

____

Date: _______________________

Today I want to remember...

____

____

____

____

____

Date: _______________________

Today I want to remember...

____

____

____

____

Date: ______________________________

Today I want to remember...

____

____

____

____

____

Date: ______________________________

Today I want to remember...

____

____

____

____

____

Date: ______________________________

Today I want to remember...

____

____

____

____

Date: _______________________________

Today I want to remember...

____
____
____
____

Date: _______________________________

Today I want to remember...

____
____
____
____

Date: _______________________________

Today I want to remember...

____
____
____

Date: _______________________________

Today I want to remember...

____

____

____

____

Date: _______________________________

Today I want to remember...

____

____

____

____

Date: _______________________________

Today I want to remember...

____

____

____

____

Date: _______________________

Today I want to remember...

____

____

____

____

Date: _______________________

Today I want to remember...

____

____

____

____

Date: _______________________

Today I want to remember...

____

____

____

____

Date: _______________________

Today I want to remember...

____

____

____

____

Date: _______________________

Today I want to remember...

____

____

____

____

Date: _______________________

Today I want to remember...

____

____

____

____

Date: _______________________

Today I want to remember...

____

____

____

____

Date: _______________________

Today I want to remember...

____

____

____

____

Date: _______________________

Today I want to remember...

____

____

____

____

Date: _______________

Today I want to remember...

____
____
____
____

Date: _______________

Today I want to remember...

____
____
____
____

Date: _______________

Today I want to remember...

____
____
____
____

Date: _______________________

Today I want to remember...

____

____

____

____

____

Date: _______________________

Today I want to remember...

____

____

____

____

____

Date: _______________________

Today I want to remember...

____

____

____

____

____

Date: _______________________

Today I want to remember...

____

____

____

____

Date: _______________________

Today I want to remember...

____

____

____

____

Date: _______________________

Today I want to remember...

____

____

____

____

Date: _______________________________

Today I want to remember...

____

____

____

____

____

Date: _______________________________

Today I want to remember...

____

____

____

____

____

Date: _______________________________

Today I want to remember...

____

____

____

____

Date: _______________________________

Today I want to remember...

____

____

____

____

Date: _______________________________

Today I want to remember...

____

____

____

____

Date: _______________________________

Today I want to remember...

____

____

____

____

Date: _______________________________

Today I want to remember...

____

____

____

____

Date: _______________________________

Today I want to remember...

____

____

____

____

Date: _______________________________

Today I want to remember...

____

____

____

____

Date: ______________________________

Today I want to remember...

____
____
____
____

Date: ______________________________

Today I want to remember...

____
____
____
____

Date: ______________________________

Today I want to remember...

____
____
____
____

Date: ____

Today I want to remember...

____

____

____

____

____

Date: ____

Today I want to remember...

____

____

____

____

____

Date: ____

Today I want to remember...

____

____

____

____

Date: _______________________

Today I want to remember...

____

____

____

____

Date: _______________________

Today I want to remember...

____

____

____

____

Date: _______________________

Today I want to remember...

____

____

____

____

Date: _______________________

Today I want to remember...

____

____

____

____

____

Date: _______________________

Today I want to remember...

____

____

____

____

____

Date: _______________________

Today I want to remember...

____

____

____

____

Date: ______________________________

Today I want to remember...

____
____
____
____

Date: ______________________________

Today I want to remember...

____
____
____
____
____

Date: ______________________________

Today I want to remember...

____
____
____
____

Date: _______________________________

Today I want to remember...

____

____

____

____

Date: _______________________________

Today I want to remember...

____

____

____

____

Date: _______________________________

Today I want to remember...

____

____

____

____

Date: ________________________________

Today I want to remember...

____

____

____

____

____

Date: ________________________________

Today I want to remember...

____

____

____

____

____

Date: ________________________________

Today I want to remember...

____

____

____

____

Date: ______________________

Today I want to remember...

____

____

____

____

____

Date: ______________________

Today I want to remember...

____

____

____

____

____

Date: ______________________

Today I want to remember...

____

____

____

____

Date: _______________________

Today I want to remember...

____

____

____

____

Date: _______________________

Today I want to remember...

____

____

____

____

Date: _______________________

Today I want to remember...

____

____

____

____

Date: _______________________

Today I want to remember...

____

____

____

____

Date: _______________________

Today I want to remember...

____

____

____

____

Date: _______________________

Today I want to remember...

____

____

____

Date: _______________________________

Today I want to remember...

____

____

____

____

____

Date: _______________________________

Today I want to remember...

____

____

____

____

____

Date: _______________________________

Today I want to remember...

____

____

____

____

Date: _______________________

Today I want to remember...

____
____
____
____

Date: _______________________

Today I want to remember...

____
____
____
____

Date: _______________________

Today I want to remember...

____
____
____

Date: _______________________

Today I want to remember...

____

____

____

____

Date: _______________________

Today I want to remember...

____

____

____

____

____

Date: _______________________

Today I want to remember...

____

____

____

____

Date: _______________________

Today I want to remember...

____

____

____

____

____

Date: _______________________

Today I want to remember...

____

____

____

____

____

Date: _______________________

Today I want to remember...

____

____

____

____

____

Date: _______________________

Today I want to remember...

____

____

____

____

Date: _______________________

Today I want to remember...

____

____

____

____

Date: _______________________

Today I want to remember...

____

____

____

____

Date: _______________________

Today I want to remember...

____

____

____

____

____

Date: _______________________

Today I want to remember...

____

____

____

____

____

Date: _______________________

Today I want to remember...

____

____

____

____

Date: _______________________

Today I want to remember...

____

____

____

____

Date: _______________________

Today I want to remember...

____

____

____

____

Date: _______________________

Today I want to remember...

____

____

____

Date: _______________________

Today I want to remember...

____

____

____

____

Date: _______________________

Today I want to remember...

____

____

____

____

Date: _______________________

Today I want to remember...

____

____

____

____

Date: _______________________________

Today I want to remember...

____
____
____
____
____

Date: _______________________________

Today I want to remember...

____
____
____
____
____

Date: _______________________________

Today I want to remember...

____
____
____
____

Date: ______________________________

Today I want to remember...

____

____

____

____

Date: ______________________________

Today I want to remember...

____

____

____

____

____

Date: ______________________________

Today I want to remember...

____

____

____

____

Date: _______________________

Today I want to remember...

____

____

____

____

Date: _______________________

Today I want to remember...

____

____

____

____

Date: _______________________

Today I want to remember...

____

____

____

____

Date: _______________________

Today I want to remember...

____

____

____

____

Date: _______________________

Today I want to remember...

____

____

____

____

Date: _______________________

Today I want to remember...

____

____

____

____

Date: _______________________________

Today I want to remember...

____

____

____

____

Date: _______________________________

Today I want to remember...

____

____

____

____

Date: _______________________________

Today I want to remember...

____

____

____

____

Date: _______________________

Today I want to remember...

____

____

____

____

Date: _______________________

Today I want to remember...

____

____

____

____

Date: _______________________

Today I want to remember...

____

____

____

____

Date: _______________________

Today I want to remember...

____
____
____
____

Date: _______________________

Today I want to remember...

____
____
____
____

Date: _______________________

Today I want to remember...

____
____
____
____

Date: _______________________________

Today I want to remember...

____

____

____

____

Date: _______________________________

Today I want to remember...

____

____

____

____

Date: _______________________________

Today I want to remember...

____

____

____

____

Date: _______________________

Today I want to remember...

____

____

____

____

____

Date: _______________________

Today I want to remember...

____

____

____

____

____

Date: _______________________

Today I want to remember...

____

____

____

____

Date: _______________________________

Today I want to remember...

____

____

____

____

Date: _______________________________

Today I want to remember...

____

____

____

____

____

Date: _______________________________

Today I want to remember...

____

____

____

____

Date: _______________________

Today I want to remember...

____

____

____

____

____

Date: _______________________

Today I want to remember...

____

____

____

____

____

Date: _______________________

Today I want to remember...

____

____

____

____

Date: _______________________________

Today I want to remember...

____

____

____

____

Date: _______________________________

Today I want to remember...

____

____

____

____

Date: _______________________________

Today I want to remember...

____

____

____

____

Date: _______________________________

Today I want to remember...

____

____

____

____

Date: _______________________________

Today I want to remember...

____

____

____

____

Date: _______________________________

Today I want to remember...

____

____

____

____

Date: _______________________

Today I want to remember...

____

____

____

____

Date: _______________________

Today I want to remember...

____

____

____

____

Date: _______________________

Today I want to remember...

____

____

____

____

Date: ______________________________

Today I want to remember...

____

____

____

____

____

Date: ______________________________

Today I want to remember...

____

____

____

____

____

Date: ______________________________

Today I want to remember...

____

____

____

____

Date: _______________________________

Today I want to remember...

____

____

____

____

____

Date: _______________________________

Today I want to remember...

____

____

____

____

____

Date: _______________________________

Today I want to remember...

____

____

____

____

Date: _______________________

Today I want to remember...

____

____

____

____

Date: _______________________

Today I want to remember...

____

____

____

____

Date: _______________________

Today I want to remember...

____

____

____

Date: _______________________

Today I want to remember...

____

____

____

____

Date: _______________________

Today I want to remember...

____

____

____

____

Date: _______________________

Today I want to remember...

____

____

____

____

Date: _______________________________

Today I want to remember...

____

____

____

____

____

Date: _______________________________

Today I want to remember...

____

____

____

____

____

Date: _______________________________

Today I want to remember...

____

____

____

____

____

Date: _______________________________

Today I want to remember...

____

____

____

____

Date: _______________________________

Today I want to remember...

____

____

____

____

Date: _______________________________

Today I want to remember...

____

____

____

____

Date: _______________________

Today I want to remember...

____

____

____

____

____

Date: _______________________

Today I want to remember...

____

____

____

____

____

Date: _______________________

Today I want to remember...

____

____

____

____

Date: _______________________

Today I want to remember...

____

____

____

____

____

Date: _______________________

Today I want to remember...

____

____

____

____

____

Date: _______________________

Today I want to remember...

____

____

____

____

Date: ______________________________

Today I want to remember...

____
____
____
____
____

Date: ______________________________

Today I want to remember...

____
____
____
____
____

Date: ______________________________

Today I want to remember...

____
____
____
____

Date: _______________________

Today I want to remember...

____

____

____

____

Date: _______________________

Today I want to remember...

____

____

____

____

Date: _______________________

Today I want to remember...

____

____

____

____

Date: _______________________

Today I want to remember...

____
____
____
____
____

Date: _______________________

Today I want to remember...

____
____
____
____
____

Date: _______________________

Today I want to remember...

____
____
____
____

Date: _______________________

Today I want to remember...

____
____
____
____

Date: _______________________

Today I want to remember...

____
____
____
____

Date: _______________________

Today I want to remember...

____
____
____
____

Date: _______________________

Today I want to remember...

____

____

____

____

Date: _______________________

Today I want to remember...

____

____

____

____

Date: _______________________

Today I want to remember...

____

____

____

____

Date: _______________________

Today I want to remember...

____
____
____
____
____

Date: _______________________

Today I want to remember...

____
____
____
____
____

Date: _______________________

Today I want to remember...

____
____
____
____

Date: ________________________

Today I want to remember...

____

____

____

____

____

Date: ________________________

Today I want to remember...

____

____

____

____

____

Date: ________________________

Today I want to remember...

____

____

____

____

Date: ___________________________

Today I want to remember...

____

____

____

____

Date: ___________________________

Today I want to remember...

____

____

____

____

____

Date: ___________________________

Today I want to remember...

____

____

____

____

____

Date: ___________________

Today I want to remember...

____

____

____

____

Date: ___________________

Today I want to remember...

____

____

____

____

____

Date: ___________________

Today I want to remember...

____

____

____

____

Date: _______________________

Today I want to remember...

____

____

____

____

Date: _______________________

Today I want to remember...

____

____

____

____

____

Date: _______________________

Today I want to remember...

____

____

____

____

____

Date: _______________________________

Today I want to remember...

____
____
____
____

Date: _______________________________

Today I want to remember...

____
____
____
____
____

Date: _______________________________

Today I want to remember...

____
____
____
____

Date: _______________________

Today I want to remember...

____

____

____

____

____

Date: _______________________

Today I want to remember...

____

____

____

____

____

Date: _______________________

Today I want to remember...

____

____

____

____

Date: _______________

Today I want to remember...

____

____

____

____

____

Date: _______________

Today I want to remember...

____

____

____

____

____

Date: _______________

Today I want to remember...

____

____

____

____

Date: _______________________

Today I want to remember...

____

____

____

____

Date: _______________________

Today I want to remember...

____

____

____

____

____

Date: _______________________

Today I want to remember...

____

____

____

____

Date: ___________________

Today I want to remember...

____

____

____

____

Date: ___________________

Today I want to remember...

____

____

____

____

Date: ___________________

Today I want to remember...

____

____

____

____

Date: _______________________________

Today I want to remember...

____

____

____

____

Date: _______________________________

Today I want to remember...

____

____

____

____

Date: _______________________________

Today I want to remember...

____

____

____

____

Date: ___________________________

Today I want to remember...

____

____

____

____

____

Date: ___________________________

Today I want to remember...

____

____

____

____

____

Date: ___________________________

Today I want to remember...

____

____

____

____

Date: _______________________________________

Today I want to remember...

____

____

____

____

____

Date: _______________________________________

Today I want to remember...

____

____

____

____

____

Date: _______________________________________

Today I want to remember...

____

____

____

____

Date: _______________________

Today I want to remember...

____

____

____

____

Date: _______________________

Today I want to remember...

____

____

____

____

Date: _______________________

Today I want to remember...

____

____

____

____

Date: ___________________________

Today I want to remember...

____

____

____

____

____

Date: ___________________________

Today I want to remember...

____

____

____

____

____

Date: ___________________________

Today I want to remember...

____

____

____

____

____

Date: _______________________

Today I want to remember...

____

____

____

____

Date: _______________________

Today I want to remember...

____

____

____

____

Date: _______________________

Today I want to remember...

____

____

____

____

Date: _______________

Today I want to remember...

____

____

____

____

Date: _______________

Today I want to remember...

____

____

____

____

Date: _______________

Today I want to remember...

____

____

____

____

Date: _______________________________

Today I want to remember...

____

____

____

____

Date: _______________________________

Today I want to remember...

____

____

____

____

Date: _______________________________

Today I want to remember...

____

____

____

____

Date: _______________________

Today I want to remember...

____

____

____

____

____

Date: _______________________

Today I want to remember...

____

____

____

____

____

Date: _______________________

Today I want to remember...

____

____

____

____

Date: ___________________________

Today I want to remember...

____

____

____

____

Date: ___________________________

Today I want to remember...

____

____

____

____

Date: ___________________________

Today I want to remember...

____

____

____

____

Date: _______________________

Today I want to remember...

____

____

____

____

Date: _______________________

Today I want to remember...

____

____

____

____

Date: _______________________

Today I want to remember...

____

____

____

____

Date: _______________________

Today I want to remember...

____

____

____

____

Date: _______________________

Today I want to remember...

____

____

____

____

____

Date: _______________________

Today I want to remember...

____

____

____

____

Date: _______________________________

Today I want to remember...

____

____

____

____

____

Date: _______________________________

Today I want to remember...

____

____

____

____

____

Date: _______________________________

Today I want to remember...

____

____

____

____

Date: _______________________

Today I want to remember...

____

____

____

____

Date: _______________________

Today I want to remember...

____

____

____

____

Date: _______________________

Today I want to remember...

____

____

____

Date: _______________________

Today I want to remember...

____
____
____
____
____

Date: _______________________

Today I want to remember...

____
____
____
____
____

Date: _______________________

Today I want to remember...

____
____
____
____

Date: _______________________

Today I want to remember...

____

____

____

____

____

Date: _______________________

Today I want to remember...

____

____

____

____

____

Date: _______________________

Today I want to remember...

____

____

____

____

Date: _______________________

Today I want to remember...

____
____
____
____

Date: _______________________

Today I want to remember...

____
____
____
____

Date: _______________________

Today I want to remember...

____
____
____
____

Date: _______________________

Today I want to remember...

____

____

____

____

Date: _______________________

Today I want to remember...

____

____

____

____

Date: _______________________

Today I want to remember...

____

____

____

____

Date: _______________________

Today I want to remember...

____

____

____

____

Date: _______________________

Today I want to remember...

____

____

____

____

Date: _______________________

Today I want to remember...

____

____

____

____

Date: _______________________

Today I want to remember...

____

____

____

____

Date: _______________________

Today I want to remember...

____

____

____

____

Date: _______________________

Today I want to remember...

____

____

____

____

Date: _______________________

Today I want to remember...

____

____

____

____

____

Date: _______________________

Today I want to remember...

____

____

____

____

____

Date: _______________________

Today I want to remember...

____

____

____

____

Date: _______________________

Today I want to remember...

____

____

____

____

Date: _______________________

Today I want to remember...

____

____

____

____

Date: _______________________

Today I want to remember...

____

____

____

____

Date: _______________________

Today I want to remember...

____

____

____

____

Date: _______________________

Today I want to remember...

____

____

____

____

Date: _______________________

Today I want to remember...

____

____

____

____

Date: _______________________

Today I want to remember...

____

____

____

____

____

Date: _______________________

Today I want to remember...

____

____

____

____

____

Date: _______________________

Today I want to remember...

____

____

____

____

Date: _______________________

Today I want to remember...

____

____

____

____

Date: _______________________

Today I want to remember...

____

____

____

____

Date: _______________________

Today I want to remember...

____

____

____

____

Date: _______________________

Today I want to remember...

____

____

____

____

Date: _______________________

Today I want to remember...

____

____

____

____

Date: _______________________

Today I want to remember...

____

____

____

____

Date: _______________________

Today I want to remember...

____

____

____

____

Date: _______________________

Today I want to remember...

____

____

____

____

Date: _______________________

Today I want to remember...

____

____

____

____

Date: _______________________

Today I want to remember...

____

____

____

____

____

Date: _______________________

Today I want to remember...

____

____

____

____

____

Date: _______________________

Today I want to remember...

____

____

____

____

Date: _______________________

Today I want to remember...

____

____

____

____

____

Date: _______________________

Today I want to remember...

____

____

____

____

____

Date: _______________________

Today I want to remember...

____

____

____

____

Date: ___________________________

Today I want to remember...

____

____

____

____

Date: ___________________________

Today I want to remember...

____

____

____

____

____

Date: ___________________________

Today I want to remember...

____

____

____

____

Date: _______________________

Today I want to remember...

____

____

____

____

Date: _______________________

Today I want to remember...

____

____

____

____

Date: _______________________

Today I want to remember...

____

____

____

____

Date: ___________________________________

Today I want to remember...

____

____

____

____

____

Date: ___________________________________

Today I want to remember...

____

____

____

____

____

Date: ___________________________________

Today I want to remember...

____

____

____

____

Date: _______________

Today I want to remember...

____

____

____

____

____

Date: _______________

Today I want to remember...

____

____

____

____

____

Date: _______________

Today I want to remember...

____

____

____

____

Date: _______________________

Today I want to remember...

____

____

____

____

Date: _______________________

Today I want to remember...

____

____

____

____

Date: _______________________

Today I want to remember...

____

____

____

____

"The trick is to enjoy life.
Don't wish away your days waiting
for better ones ahead."

Marjorie Pay Hinkley

www.ingramcontent.com/pod-product-compliance
Lightning Source LLC
Chambersburg PA
CBHW021549150726
47990CB00006B/2457